JAPAN

A Modern Land with Ancient Roots

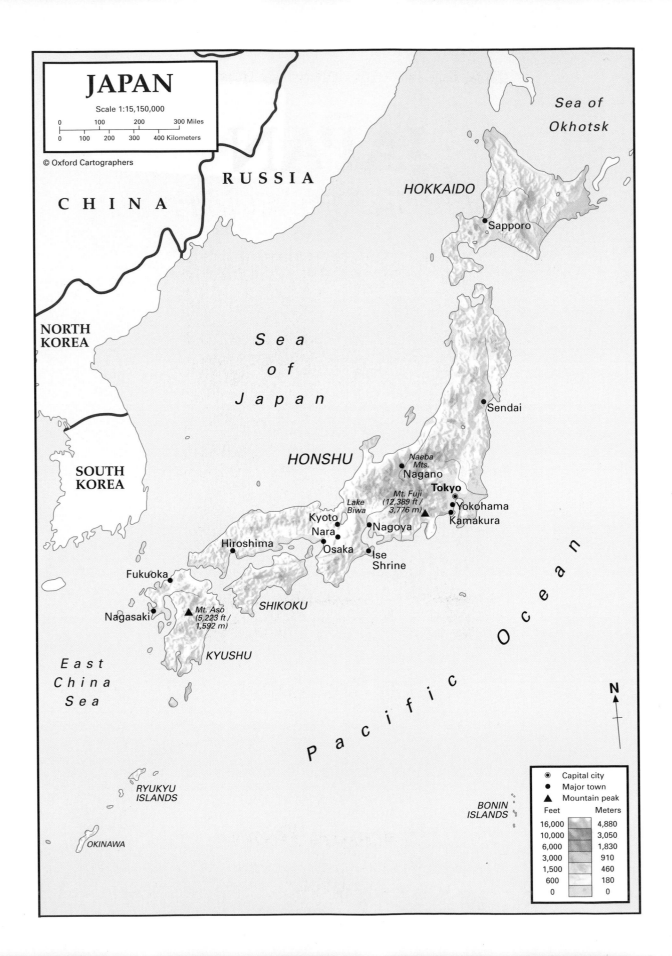

JAPAN

Scale 1:15,150,000

0   100   200   300 Miles
0 100 200 300 400 Kilometers

© Oxford Cartographers

RUSSIA

CHINA

Sea of Okhotsk

HOKKAIDO

● Sapporo

NORTH
KOREA

SOUTH
KOREA

S e a

o f

J a p a n

● Sendai

HONSHU

Naeba Mts.
● Nagano
Tokyo ⊙

Mt. Fuji
(12,389 ft /
3,776 m) ▲

Lake Biwa

Kyoto ●
Nara ●
● Nagoya

● Yokohama
● Kamakura

Hiroshima ●

Osaka ●
● Ise Shrine

Fukuoka ●

SHIKOKU

Nagasaki ●

▲ *Mt. Asó*
(5,223 ft /
1,592 m)

KYUSHU

East
China
Sea

Pacific Ocean

RYUKYU
ISLANDS

BONIN
ISLANDS

OKINAWA

⊙ Capital city
● Major town
▲ Mountain peak

Feet	Meters
16,000	4,880
10,000	3,050
6,000	1,830
3,000	910
1,500	460
600	180
0	0

N

JAPAN
A Modern Land with Ancient Roots

Irene Flum Galvin

BENCHMARK BOOKS

MARSHALL CAVENDISH

NEW YORK

*With thanks to Yasuko Makino,
Japanese Studies Librarian, Columbia University, New York City,
for her thoughtful reading of the manuscript,
and to Takako Nakamoto and the librarians at
the Brighton Memorial Library, Rochester, New York.*

TO TOM, RACHEL, AND DANNY

Benchmark Books
Marshall Cavendish Corporation
99 White Plains Road
Tarrytown, New York 10591-9001

Library of Congress Cataloging-in-Publication Data

Galvin, Irene Flum, date.
    Japan / by Irene Flum Galvin.
        p.   cm. — (Exploring cultures of the world)
    Includes bibliographical references.
    Summary: Discusses the history, geography, daily life, culture, and customs of the island nation of Japan.
    ISBN 0-7614-0188-1 (lib. binding)
    1. Japan—Civilization—Juvenile literature.   [1. Japan.]   I. Title. II. Series.
DS821.G32   1996
952—dc20   95-15321

Printed and bound in Italy

Book design by Carol Matsuyama
Photo research by Laurie Platt Winfrey, Carousel Research, Inc.

Front cover: Japanese girls wear bright traditional kimonos at a festival.
Back cover: A woman digs for clams near the torii (gateway) of a Shinto shrine at low tide.

Photo Credits

Front cover and page 37: courtesy of Chuck Fishman/Woodfin Camp; back cover and pages 22, 38: courtesy of George Holton/Photo Researchers; title page and page 30: courtesy of Charles Gupton/Tony Stone Images; pages 6, 11: Tomomi Saito/DUNQ/Photo Researchers; pages 10, 24: Masao Hayashi/DUNQ/Photo Researchers; pages 13, 16, 23, 36, 50, 57: Hiroshi Harada/DUNQ/Photo Researchers; pages 14, 54: The Bridgeman Art Library, London; page 18: Mark Wexler/Woodfin Camp; page 20: Paul Chesley/Tony Stone Worldwide; page 25: Lindsay Hebberd/Woodfin Camp; pages 26, 52: Paolo Koch/Photo Researchers; page 28: Joan Lebold Cohen/Photo Researchers; page 32: Jose Azel/Woodfin Camp; pages 33, 35, 53: Mike Yamashita/Woodfin Camp; page 40: Allen Green/Photo Researchers; page 42: Andy Sacks/Tony Stone Worldwide; page 44: Herbert Loebil/New York Public Library, Print Room; page 47: Charles Petit, Agence Vandystadt, Paris/Photo Researchers; page 48: E. T. Archive, London

Contents

Japan is famous for its cherry trees, which blossom all over the land in the springtime.

1
GEOGRAPHY AND HISTORY

Land of Cherry Blossoms and Samurai

Gods, Goddesses, and Emperors

An old story describes how Japan was created when brother and sister gods named Izanagi (eez-uh-nah-gee) and Izanami (eez-uh-nah-mee) dipped a jeweled spear into the ocean and sprinkled saltwater drops down from the sky. These drops then became the islands of Japan.

Izanagi and Izanami also created other gods and goddesses. The sun goddess, Amaterasu, was born from Izanagi's left eye. Her brother Susano (soo-zah-noh), the god of storms, was born from his nose. When Amaterasu was chosen as the ruler of the Plain of High Heaven, Susano ruined his sister's rice fields and threw a dead horse into her palace. Amaterasu became so angry that she hid in a cave, and the world was left in darkness.

The other gods used a mirror, a crowing rooster, and singing birds to try to get Amaterasu out of the cave so the sun would shine again. They danced and laughed so loudly that Amaterasu became curious. When she peeped out, a strong god grabbed her arm and the other gods sealed off the cave so she couldn't go back in.

The sun goddess sent her grandson Ninigi (nih-nee-jee) down to earth with a magic mirror, a sword, and jewels to prove he was a god and had the right to rule Japan. According to the story, Ninigi's *grandson, Jimmu Tenno, became the first human emperor in 660 B.C. Since Jimmu Tenno, there have been 125 emperors in Japan—the longest unbroken line of emperors in the world.*

AMATERASU AND JAPAN

The sun goddess Amaterasu is still worshiped today at Ise (ee-say) Shrine on Honshu Island. Even Japan's name is related to the sun goddess: The word for *Japan* in Japanese is *Nippon* or *Nihon*—"The Land of the Rising Sun." Japan has also had many other names. In ancient myths the country was known as the Land of Fresh Rice Ears of a Thousand Autumns and the Land of Abundant Reed Plains.

A Country of Islands

The islands that make up Japan did come from the sea, though scientists say they were created by violent movements under the earth, not from the spear of a god. Millions of years ago, volcanic eruptions shoved gigantic mountains up out of the sea. The tops of the mountains became the islands of Japan.

Japan is made up of four large islands and 3,900 smaller ones. The four main islands, from largest to smallest, are Honshu, Hokkaido, Kyushu, and Shikoku. If all the islands were squeezed together, Japan would be about the size of California.

The islands of Japan lie in the Pacific Ocean off the northeastern coast of Asia in the shape of a big smile or half-moon. From north to south, Japan is 1,865 miles (3,003 kilometers) long. If the four main islands were set on a map of the United States, they would stretch all the way from Maine down to northern Florida. At its broadest point, Japan is only about 250 miles (403 kilometers) wide. To the west is the Sea of Japan and to the east is the Pacific Ocean. No part of the country is more than 100 miles (161 kilometers) from the sea.

Water separates Japan from all its neighbors. Korea, Japan's closest neighbor, is too far away to be seen—about 100 miles (161 kilometers) away. About 600 miles (966 kilometers) of water lie between Japan and China.

Land of Many Mountains

Mountains run down the middle of all the islands of Japan, covering about three-quarters of the land. Most of Japan's highest mountains are on Honshu, the largest island. The highest and most famous mountain on Honshu and in all Japan is Mount Fuji. The Japanese consider this spectacular peak a symbol of the beauty of their land.

Like many of Japan's mountains, Mount Fuji is a volcano, though it has not erupted since 1707. About seventy of Japan's volcanoes are active. Sometimes they spurt ashes or hot lava on the surrounding countryside, destroying homes and hurting people. The largest volcano in the world, Mount Aso, is on the southern island of Kyushu.

Besides volcanoes, the Japanese also have to watch out for earthquakes. Each year the ground shakes with about eight thousand tremors. Most are so small that people ignore them, but sometimes an earthquake is big and causes damage. In 1995 the worst earthquake in Japan in seventy years hit Kobe, a port city on Honshu. Over 5,000 people were killed, over 26,000 were injured, and more than 56,000 buildings were damaged or destroyed.

Sometimes an earthquake shakes the ocean floor. When this happens, huge sea waves called tsunami (tsoo-nah-mee) strike the land and cause great damage.

Mount Fuji, Japan's highest peak, rises beyond bright green fields of tea plantations. Mount Fuji is an ancient and famous symbol of the land of Japan. Poets have written about it, painters have painted it, and every summer hundreds of thousands of people climb it.

In spite of its many natural dangers, Japan is a beautiful land. With its long, rugged coastline, it has spectacular beaches, cliffs, and rocks. Hundreds of short, swift rivers plunge through the forest-covered mountains. Beautiful lakes nestle in the craters of volcanoes. The Japanese like to visit the beautiful places in their country and they celebrate the land's natural wonders in their poetry and painting.

Cherry Blossoms and Snow Sculptures

Most of Japan has a mild climate. In March and April the cherry trees bloom, and the country is covered with white and pink blossoms. From early June to mid-July, it is hot and rainy. The Japanese call these rains the plum rains, because they come

10

when plums are ripening on the trees. After the rains stop, the hot, humid weather lasts until the middle of September.

When autumn comes, the air grows fresh and cool, and the leaves turn red and yellow. Since Japan lies in the path of tropical storms, September also brings typhoons. These are tropical storms with heavy rains and violent winds that can cause flooding and damage to houses and crops.

Winter lasts from December to February. The Pacific side of Japan has a mild winter with sunny days and occasional snow. The northern and western parts of Japan get lots of snow. Hokkaido gets so much snow that the city of Sapporo holds a Snow Festival every February. People pile up mountains of snow and build huge snow sculptures in the shape of tigers, spaceships, peacocks, and even the Statue of Liberty.

In northern Japan, children enjoy spending cold winter evenings in snow huts like these, where they eat dinner and play games.

Natural Resources

Japan has few natural resources. The Japanese use waterpower, the sun, and nuclear power for energy, but have to import oil, coal, tin, and copper.

Because the land is so mountainous, only a small part can be used for farming. Japan produces enough rice to feed its people, but many other foods must be bought from other countries.

Where the Japanese Live

Three-quarters of the Japanese live crowded together in big cities on the flat land near the ocean in the central and southern parts of the country. Tokyo, the capital and largest city, has twelve million people. Other big cities are Yokohama, Osaka, Nagoya, Fukuoka, and Sapporo. Only one-quarter of the Japanese live in rural areas.

An Ancient People

Scientists believe the first people in Japan lived on Honshu between 8000 and 300 B.C. Little is known about them except that they lived by fishing and hunting. Around A.D. 200, invaders from Korea mixed with the original people. Large groups of related families, called clans, fought with one another for power. The most powerful clan was the Yamato clan.

In the seventh century one of Japan's leaders, Prince Shotoku, sent ambassadors to China. The Japanese learned how to weave silk, work in metals, and build ships. They also adopted the religion and philosophy of the Chinese people, and set up a strong central government with an emperor, as in China. Some years earlier the Japanese had already borrowed the Chinese system of writing. The Japanese adapted these new ways of living and working to fit their own people, language, and land.

On the Ginza, a famous street in the Japanese capital city of Tokyo, thousands of people stroll along on a Sunday, when the street has been closed to cars.

Throughout their history the Japanese have borrowed from other cultures while keeping their own ways.

In the ninth century an important family, the Fujiwaras, became more powerful than the emperor. For the next four hundred years the Fujiwaras ruled Japan. At first this was a peaceful time, when arts and literature flourished. But then wars began to break out across the country.

The wars were fought among powerful lords who owned large estates and kept armies of warriors. These warriors,

13

called samurai (sah-muh-rai), swore to be loyal to their lord, even if it meant giving up their lives. They trained to be excellent swordsmen and were feared and respected by the Japanese people.

In 1192 the most powerful lord, Yoritomo Minamoto, won control of Japan. Yoritomo became the shogun (shoh-guhn), or military dictator. He allowed the emperor to remain on the throne, but the shogun held the real power. For the next seven hundred years, Japan was ruled by shoguns. But fighting continued as one lord fought with another to be shogun.

Closing Japan's Doors to Foreigners

Unity finally came to Japan late in the sixteenth century, when a great lord, Tokugawa Ieyasu, became shogun of all Japan. Ieyasu set up his capital in Edo, as Tokyo was then called. For over 250 years, Japan was ruled by shoguns from the Tokugawa family.

The Tokugawas brought peace to Japan by making very strict laws. People were divided into four classes. The highest class was the military, which included the landholding lords and their samurai. Beneath them were the farmers, craft workers, and merchants. There were rules for everything: what kind of clothes people could wear, how many soups they could have for dinner (no more than two), and even what size doll a child could have.

The Tokugawas wanted to prevent changes that would threaten their power.

They decided that contact with foreigners was bad for their country. So in 1637 all foreigners were thrown out of Japan. For more than two hundred years, Japan was almost closed to the outside world. Japanese citizens were forbidden to go to other countries, and those living in other countries were not allowed to return home.

In medieval times, battles raged throughout the land as warlords fought for power. Here, a fleet of ships is about to attack a town.

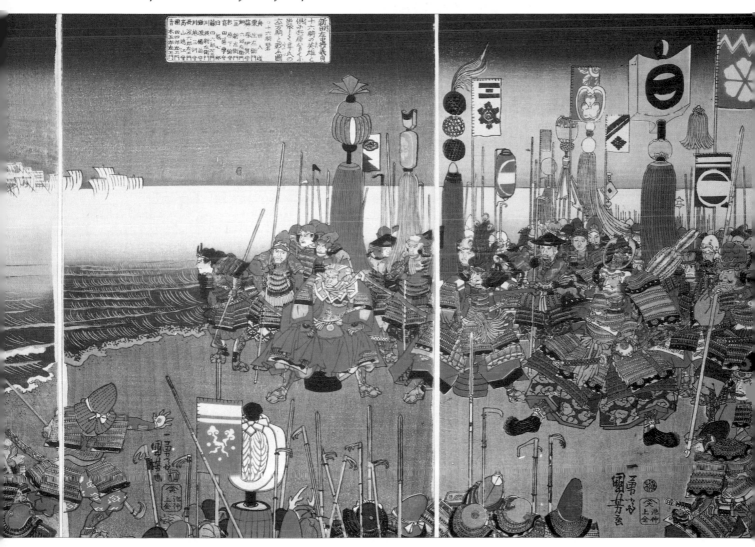

Black Ships Bring Modern Times

This old street in Tokyo looks very much the way it did during the days of the shogun, when Tokyo was known as Edo.

In 1854 Commodore Matthew Perry of the United States anchored off the coast of Japan. The shogun knew that Perry's large black battleships were more powerful than his, so he was forced to agree when the commodore asked Japan to open its doors to the world. Before long, Japan was trading with the United States, Britain, the Netherlands, and Russia.

The Tokugawa shoguns lost power in 1867 and the emperor again ruled Japan. Emperor Meiji (may-jee) realized that if Japan did not become a modern country, it might be conquered by one of Europe's powerful nations. Meiji ordered that the latest in Western technology, such as railroads and communication systems, be brought to Japan. He took away the samurais' power, made a constitution, created a modern army and navy, and started the public school system. In just fifty years, Japan became a modern nation.

As Japan modernized, it also started building an empire. It won wars against China and Russia, and took over Korea. In the 1930s the leaders of the army and navy gained control of the government. In 1937 Japan went to war against China again.

JAPANESE GOVERNMENT

Japan has a form of government known as a constitutional monarchy. The emperor is the symbol of the nation but has no powers related to government. The present emperor, Akihito, came to the throne in 1989.

The head of government is the prime minister, who is the leader of the party elected to power by the people. The prime minister rules with a cabinet of ministers whom he selects from among members of the national legislature called the Diet. The current prime minister is Tomiichi Murayama.

The Diet is made up of the House of Representatives, with 511 members, and the House of Councillors, with 252 members. It is the most powerful branch of government.

The cabinet, not the prime minister, selects justices for the Supreme Court, the highest court in the nation. There is a chief justice and fourteen associate justices.

Japan is divided into forty-seven sections, called prefectures. Each has a governor. There are also village, town, and city governments.

Then, on December 7, 1941, Japan entered World War II, siding with the Germans. As its first act of war against the United States, Japan bombed the United States Navy at Pearl Harbor.

In the summer of 1945, the United States dropped two atomic bombs on the Japanese cities of Hiroshima and Nagasaki. Japan surrendered. For the next six years, American soldiers controlled Japan. Under the guidance of the American forces, the Japanese created a new constitution and became a democratic country. The constitution guaranteed freedom of speech and religion. It gave workers the right to organize unions, and women the right to vote. It also stated that the Japanese would not go to war anymore.

The United States and other countries also helped Japan rebuild its cities and industries. Today cars, electronic goods, and other products made by Japanese companies are sold all over the world. Japan has one of the strongest economies in the world and is once again a major world power.

Bowing is an age-old custom. It is a mark of courtesy to others and a sign of respect for elders—very important values in Japan.

2

THE PEOPLE

The Japanese Way

The Japanese are a blend of early settlers called the Ainu (eye-noo)—a fair-skinned people who still live in northern Japan—and yellow-skinned and brown-black people who came to Japan almost two thousand years ago from mainland Asia and islands in the Pacific. Because they were isolated from other countries for centuries, the Japanese almost never mixed with non-Japanese.

Most Japanese people have straight black hair, dark eyes, and a slender build. They all speak the same language—Japanese—and share many customs and ways of doing things.

The Japanese also share a very small living space. There are 125 million people in Japan—about half the population of the United States—in a land the size of California. All these people can live only on the 10 percent of the land without mountains. So Japan is very crowded.

Getting Along

Because they are so crowded together, the Japanese have found special ways to get along with one another. There are

TAKING THE TRAINS

Japan is so crowded that, during the Tokyo rush hour, men wearing white gloves push people into the subway trains so the doors will shut.

Riders are a lot more comfortable on Japan's Bullet Train, the *Shinkansen* (sheen-kahn-sehn). The fastest train in the world, the Bullet Train can go as fast as 160 miles (257 kilometers) an hour. It takes only about three hours to travel the 345 miles (555 kilometers) between Tokyo and Osaka—and the Bullet Train is almost always on time!

rules in Japan for just about everything. There is a "right" way to wrap presents, to use chopsticks, to arrange flowers, and to do nearly everything else. The rules are needed to keep peace and harmony among people, since they live so close together. Rules are also valued because the group—more than the individual—is considered very important, and the Japanese want everyone in the group to get along.

The Japanese feel a strong connection to their families, schools, and workplaces. If the group does well, everyone feels good. If one person does something wrong, the whole group feels bad. The rules let everyone know how to get along within the group.

One way the Japanese get along with one another is by being polite. They will hide their own feelings rather than hurt someone else's.

The Japanese bow when they say hello and good-bye and when they thank someone. Bowing is so much a part of Japanese culture that people often bow even when they talk on the telephone! The one who bows lowest, longest, and the most times is always the person with lower rank, or position. The Japanese believe that people with higher rank should be treated with respect, and bowing is one way they show it.

People are ranked according to age, sex, and social status. Older people rank higher than younger people, and men higher than women. Three minority groups have a lower social status than the rest of the Japanese.

The largest minority group is called *burakumin* (boo-rah-koo-meen), or outcasts. These are Japanese people who have jobs—or whose ancestors had jobs—involving blood and death, such as butchering. The outcasts have a hard time getting work at some companies, and are not welcomed into marriage with other Japanese.

The second minority group is people of Korean descent, some of whose ancestors came to Japan as long as four hundred years ago. The third group is the Ainu, the first inhabitants of Japan. Like Native Americans in the United States, many Ainu were pushed out of their land. These three groups struggle for their right to be treated the same as other Japanese.

Blending Religious Traditions

Most Japanese say they aren't religious, but they still practice the two main religions in Japan: Shinto and Buddhism.

Shinto, which means the "way of the gods," is Japan's

The ancestors of this Ainu man were the first people to live in Japan.
Over the years many were pushed off their lands. Today fewer than twenty
thousand Ainu people remain, most on the northern island of Hokkaido.

oldest religion. The early Japanese believed there were gods or spirits in trees, mountains, and all of nature. They worshiped these spirits and believed in living in harmony with nature. The Japanese also honor their ancestors and heroes as part of the Shinto religion.

Today there are over ninety thousand Shinto shrines in

Japan. Before going into a shrine, people purify themselves by washing their hands and mouths. Worshipers clap their hands to get the attention of the gods, bow to show respect, and offer food and money to them. Many homes also have a small altar where food is offered to the gods and to relatives who have died.

Japan's other main religion, Buddhism, began in India and was introduced to Japan by traveling Korean monks in the sixth century. Buddhist temples have statues of Buddha, a re-markable teacher who founded the religion. The Great Buddha

This Shinto shrine, like thousands of others in Japan, is identified by a gateway called a torii.

The Gold Pavilion, a Buddhist temple, stands in the perfect stillness of a beautiful lake in Kyoto.

in the Todaiji Temple in Nara is the largest statue of Buddha in Japan. It is 53 feet (16 meters) tall and made of 437 tons (396 tonnes) of bronze, 286 pounds (129 kilograms) of pure gold, 165 pounds (74 kilograms) of mercury, and 7 tons (6 tonnes) of vegetable wax.

The form of Buddhism that has most affected the Japanese way of life is Zen Buddhism. Zen teaches self-discipline as a way of balancing the mind, body, and spirit. It also emphasizes simplicity and meditation to become at peace with oneself and the world.

Buddhism has greatly influenced Japanese customs, arts, and attitudes. The discipline and simplicity of Zen is seen today in almost every Japanese art.

Another philosophy that has influenced Japanese culture is Confucianism, a system of thoughts and beliefs that came from China and Korea in the fifth century. Confucianism stresses the importance of right behavior and fulfilling one's duty to those higher on the social ladder. This philosophy contributed greatly to the Japanese respect for obedience, loyalty, and clearly defined rules.

About 1 percent of the Japanese are Christian. In recent years, Christian-style wedding ceremonies have become popular among many Japanese, even when they are not Christian.

The Great Buddha in the Todaiji Temple is famous for its enormous size and weight.

The genius of the Japanese for blending different customs and making them their own is clear in their approach to religion: Many Japanese follow Shinto rituals at shrines, Western customs when they marry, and Buddhist funeral rites when they die.

Ancient traditions find a place in modern Japan, as a Shinto priest blesses a car. After purifying the car with salt, the priest uses a broom to whisk away evil spirits.

Working, Japanese-Style

In the past most Japanese worked as farmers. Today only 15 percent are farmers. Most people work in factories, making computers, cameras, television sets, cars, and other products. More than 400,000 people are employed in Japan's fishing industry. Others work as salespeople, doctors, engineers, teachers, scientists, construction workers, artists—the same kinds of jobs found in other countries.

Most Japanese work six days a week. The workday is very

SAY IT IN JAPANESE

Here is how you would say some common words and phrases in Japanese.

Hello (on meeting)	*Konnichi wa* (koh-nee-chee wah)
Hello? (on phone)	*Moshi, moshi?* (moh-shee, moh-shee)
Good morning	*Ohayo gozaimasu* (oh-high-yoh goh-zai-mahs)
Yes	*Hai* (hai)
No	*Iie* (ee-eh)
Please (when offering something)	*Do-zo* (dough-zoh)
Thank you	*Arigato gozaimasu* (ah-ree-gah-toh goh-zai-mahs)
I'm sorry	*Sumimasen* (soo-mee-mah-sehn)
What's your name?	*Onamae wa?* (oh-nah-mah-ay wah)
Good-bye	*Sayonara* (sai-yoh-nah-rah)

long: In the Tokyo area, people often travel two or three hours a day to get to work, and are also expected to work overtime. In the best companies, workers are promised lifelong jobs, health care, and housing, so they are willing to work extra hard to keep their employers happy. In many cases the boss is seen as a friend and a teacher, not just as a boss. Sometimes the boss even arranges dates for unmarried workers!

Companies often have parties, trips, and outings. In the morning, workers may exercise together, and after work, they often spend time together drinking and singing. But many younger Japanese no longer feel the same loyalty to their companies as the older generation. They want to spend more time

The traditional Japanese robe, the kimono, is still worn on special occasions, like festivals and weddings.

with their families or having fun, rather than devote their whole lives to work.

An increasing number of women work outside the home. Because companies expect employees to work long hours of overtime, women with family responsibilities cannot compete with male employees. Few women have responsible positions in companies or in government. Attitudes change slowly, and women in Japan often accept the roles they have been given.

Blue Jeans and Kimonos

Most Japanese wear Western-style clothes at home, school, and work. Men and women wear suits and dresses, and young people wear blue jeans, T-shirts, and sneakers.

The kimono (kuh-moh-noh) is a traditional Japanese robe sometimes worn for special occasions such as festivals and weddings. Girls wear bright colors like red or blue, women wear quieter colors, and boys and men wear dark blue or brown. The obi (oh-bee) is a long, broad sash worn with the kimono. Different-colored obis are worn in each season: In spring they may have a plum-blossom design and in autumn, red maple.

Both men and women wear cotton kimonos called *yukata* (yoo-kah-tah) in the summer. The *yukata* is light colored and lightweight so the wearer can keep cool on hot, humid days. As always in Japan, there is a "right" way to wear the *yukata*: The left side must be tucked over the right. If the right side is tucked over, it is a symbol of death.

Maybe most of the Japanese do wear their *yukata* the "right" way. They live longer than any other people in the world: women an average of eighty-two years and men, seventy-six years.

A family gathers for dinner. Although Japanese families are smaller these days than they used to be, the family as a group is still very important.

3
FAMILY LIFE, FESTIVALS, AND FOOD

Days of Celebration

Children are loved so much in Japan that there is a nick-name for them— "child treasures." When they are very young, they are almost never left alone or with baby-sitters. Mothers keep babies close by carrying them on their backs, and young children often sleep with their parents.

Family First

The family as a group is very important in Japan—more than the individual members of the family. Children are taught that bad behavior disgraces the family, and that they should respect and obey parents and ancestors. By the age of six, children are expected to be responsible and work hard in school to represent their families the best they can.

The man is the head of the household in Japan. Most Japanese believe that men should work and women should stay at home and care for their husband and children. More women work outside the home today than in the past, but they are not given promotions or paid the same as men are.

Retired grandparents often live with their eldest son and his family. However, this is not as common as it used to be because apartments are so small and sometimes families live in different cities. Families have fewer children, too: only one or two, compared to years ago when the average was three or four.

A "child treasure" stays close to Mother.

Japanese-Style Homes

Some families live in large, traditional houses. These houses, with two stories and large, airy rooms, are found mostly in the countryside. But most people live in the crowded cities. Because land is so scarce, Japanese apartments and houses are expensive and smaller than those in the United States.

The Japanese never wear shoes in their homes. They leave their shoes in the hallway—facing out, to make it easy to put them on again—and wear slippers called *surippa* (soor-ee-puh). Many of the floors are covered with woven straw mats called tatami (tah-tah-mee). Before going into a room with tatami, people take their slippers off too, to keep the tatami clean.

There is less furniture in most Japanese homes than in American homes. This gives the rooms an open, clean feeling. In traditional Japanese rooms, there are no chairs—people sit on cushions at low tables. Most homes do not have central heating, so during the cold months, people like to sit with their feet under the *kotatsu* (koh-taht-soo), a table with a heater under it. Families often sit around the *kotatsu* in the evening, reading, eating, or watching television.

The Japanese sleep on quilted mattresses called futons (foo-tahns), which they spread on the floor at night. In the morning they roll up the futons and put them away in the closet. This way the same room can serve as bedroom and living

This room in a traditional Japanese house looks quiet and peaceful—proba-bly because it has little furniture. The Japanese sit on cushions rather than chairs, and they adorn their homes simply, with natural things like flowers.

33

room. Paper-covered screens called shoji (shoh-jee) slide back and forth to make different rooms out of a single area.

Many Japanese homes have a small Buddhist altar where the family brings offerings of food to honor the memory of their ancestors. Some also have a tokonoma (toh-kuh-noh-mah), a small area decorated simply and beautifully with a vase of flowers and a scroll painting.

Most rooms are furnished in the Japanese style, but sometimes one room has Western-style furniture such as couches, tables, and chairs. Most families have modern conveniences like television sets, radios, stereos, and computers.

In a Japanese home, the toilet room is separate from the bathroom. There are special toilet slippers to wear in the toilet room. When you come out, you have to remember to switch back into your regular slippers.

Bathing in Japan is different from bathing in the United States. The Japanese actually take two baths at a time. First they soap up and wash off outside the tub. The bathroom has a drain in the floor, so it's all right to get water all over. Then when they're clean, they get into the bathtub—without soap—to relax in the clean, hot water. Afterward, they don't let the water out: Everyone in the family shares the same clean water.

There are also public baths in Japan. Many people soak and relax in the same large tub, which is more like a pool.

The Japanese love gardens, even if they only have small ones. People in apartments sometimes joke that their garden is no bigger than a cat's forehead—but they love it anyway.

Festivals and Fun

The Japanese love festivals. Almost every day there's a festival going on somewhere in the country. Some are religious cele-

A group of men relax in one of the many public baths in Japan.

brations, while others celebrate the coming of a new season or the blossoming of certain flowers. People carry portable shrines in parades. They dance and play drums, flutes, and bells. Some Japanese like to wear kimonos on festival days.

New Year's, called O-shogatsu (oh shoh-gaht-soo), is the biggest festival of all. People get ready for the holiday by cleaning their houses and paying off their debts so they can start the new year fresh. They decorate their homes and streets with pine branches (for strength and long life), bamboo stalks (for strong character), and straw ropes (for good luck and to drive away evil spirits). They also send New Year's cards, which are all delivered at one time on New Year's Day.

On New Year's Eve many people visit temples and shrines. At midnight, temple bells ring 108 times to welcome the new year. On New Year's Day, families dress in their best clothes and visit the homes of relatives and friends. Children receive

On the eve of spring, Japanese celebrate with a bean-scattering ceremony at a Shinto shrine.

gifts of money in red envelopes, and older people play an ancient card game called Songs of a Hundred Poets, in which they have to match the first lines of a poem with the last verses.

On March 3, Japanese girls celebrate the Dolls' Festival, or Hina Matsuri (hee-nah maht-soor-ee). They set special dolls in ancient costumes on stands covered with red cloth, along with miniature furniture and food. There are usually fifteen dolls representing the emperor and empress, court ladies, and musicians. Peach blossoms, which stand for gentleness and happiness in marriage, also decorate the stands. Girls invite their friends over to see their doll collections and to eat special rice cakes and sing songs.

Children's Day, or Kodomo-no-hi (koh-doh-moh noh hee), is a national holiday celebrated on May 5. Families fly colorful paper or cloth streamers from bamboo poles outside their homes. The streamers are shaped like carp, a fish considered to be brave and strong, because families hope their children will be as determined as the carp.

Another festival, Seven-Five-Three Day, or Shichi-go-san (shee-chee goh sahn), is celebrated because a long time ago people thought the numbers three, five, and seven were unlucky. On November 15, families bring girls who are seven,

Girls wear bright traditional kimonos, and makeup, at a New Year's celebration.

boys who are five, and both girls and boys who are three years old to a shrine to thank the gods for their good health and to ask for blessings for continued growth.

Rice and Green Tea

Rice is such an important food in Japan that the names of the meals all have rice in them: breakfast, or *asa-gohan,* "morning rice"; lunch, or *hiru-gohan,* "noon rice"; and supper, or *ban-gohan,* "night rice." Almost every meal includes rice and the national drink, green tea, which is served hot without anything added to it.

But the Japanese eat many kinds of food besides rice. A typ-

Buddhist monks celebrate the Festival of the Ages at a temple in Kyoto.

RULES FOR EATING WITH CHOPSTICKS

1. Before the Japanese pick up their chopsticks to begin a meal, they bow their heads and say, *"Itadakimasu"* (ee-tah-dah-kee-mahs). This means "I receive," and is a way of saying thanks for the food.

2. Don't stick your chopsticks upright in your rice. This is the way rice is offered to the dead in the family shrine.

3. To take food from the same serving dish as others, turn the chopsticks around and use the ends that haven't been in your mouth.

4. Don't grab chopsticks with your fist, wave them in the air or over the food, stick them into a piece of food, use them to pass food from person to person, or dig through a shared dish to find the best piece.

5. When you finish, put your chopsticks neatly on the chopstick rest, a tiny dish sometimes shaped like a fish or flower. If there is no chopstick rest, place the chopsticks across the dish closest to you.

ical breakfast might be miso (mee-soh) soup (made of soybean paste), rice, and pickled vegetables—but eggs and toast are popular, too. For lunch or dinner, thick wheat noodles called udon (ooh-dahn) and thin buckwheat noodles called soba are popular, as is sushi (soo-shee)—bite-size cakes of vinegared rice with raw fish (or other seafood or vegetables) dipped in soy sauce.

Other favorite foods are sashimi (sliced raw fish), tempura, (fried seafood and vegetables), seaweed, tofu (bean curd), and pickled vegetables. Japanese children also enjoy hamburgers, pizza, pancakes, and other foods common in the West.

In Japan the way food looks is as important as its freshness and taste. Food is served on small dishes on a tray and is eaten with chopsticks. Forks, knives, and spoons are used only in Western-style restaurants. How do you eat soup without a spoon? Fish the solids out with your chopsticks and then pick up the bowl and sip the broth. It's all right to slurp your soup—it's considered a sign of a good appetite!

Schoolgirls enjoy a "box" lunch.

4

SCHOOL AND RECREATION

Studying Hard and Having Fun

Schoolchildren in Japan study very hard. As early as nursery school, competition begins to get into the best kindergarten, the best elementary school, the best high school, and finally, the best university. Each school has its own entrance exam, and the exams for the best schools are very difficult. The hardest exams are the college entrance exams. Because graduates of the top universities are assured excellent jobs, everyone wants to go to Tokyo University or one of the other half-dozen highest-ranked schools.

To prepare for all these exams, many children go to private schools called "cram schools" after school, in the evenings, and on the weekends. After they get into the university, life is easier—students don't have to work as hard, and few fail.

A Long School Year

Children are required to attend school from ages six to fifteen. But many begin earlier, at age three or four, and almost everyone stays until age eighteen. Elementary school is from ages six to twelve, followed by three years of middle school and three years of high school. Over a third of these students then go on to college.

The school year is from April to March, with six weeks of vacation in the summer. Japanese children go to school 240 days a year, compared to 180 days in the United States. School is from 8:30 A.M. to about 3:00 P.M. Monday through Friday, plus a half day on Saturday.

Despite the high standards of education in Japan, these fourth-graders manage to have fun in class.

Uniforms and Working Together

Elementary schools may have as many as forty children in one class. In private elementary schools, middle school, and high school, children wear uniforms. Girls usually wear jackets with white blouses and pleated navy blue skirts. Boys wear black pants and jackets with brass buttons and stand-up collars.

Children call their teachers *sensei* (sehn-say), which means "master" and is a sign of respect.

Children and teachers work together to take care of their school. Groups take turns cleaning the room, halls, and bathrooms. If the school has a garden, the students plant and take care of the flowers, too.

A typical school week for a ten-year-old includes math, science, social studies, Japanese, art, music, physical education, morals (the study of right behavior), and calligraphy (the art of writing Japanese). All students begin to study English in middle school and most continue to study it through high school.

After the school day, students may take private lessons in piano, abacus (a counting device), or swimming, or they may go to a "cram school" to study Japanese and math. Then there is homework: Even elementary school children get as much as five or six hours of homework a night.

The Japanese Language

Learning to read and write Japanese takes a great deal of time and concentration. The language is written with three kinds of symbols. The first are Chinese characters, or *kanji* (kahn-jee), which were brought to Japan in the fifth century and adapted to the Japanese language. There were many differences between Chinese and Japanese, so two other writing systems were created—*hiragana* (hee-rah-gahn-ah) and *katakana* (kah-tah-kah-nah). Each has forty-eight symbols, which stand for syllables, not single letters. They are used to spell out words that cannot be written with *kanji*

Kanji are used to express ideas. Some are very complicated—one *kanji* may have as many as thirty brush strokes! Each stroke must be written in the correct order and direction.

43

The Japanese character yo, *part of the* katakana *writing system, takes the form of an owl in this woodblock print.*

There are over two thousand *kanji* in everyday use. Educated Japanese know about five to ten thousand *kanji*.

By the time they finish high school, Japanese children must know how to read and write 1,850 *kanji* plus the 48 *katakana* and 48 *hiragana*. Even though it is hard to learn written Japanese, 99 percent of the Japanese can read and write. It's easy to see why elementary-school students spend more time studying Japanese than anything else!

Playtime

When they are not studying, Japanese children like to watch television, play Nintendo (a Japanese invention) and computer games, read comic books, or play with their friends. Sometimes they fly kites or spin tops.

Origami is also a popular hobby and art. Children fold squares of colored paper into birds, lions, dogs, and hundreds of other shapes. The crane, a wading bird, is the most popular shape. The Japanese believe the crane is a symbol of long life. Folding and stringing together a thousand cranes is believed to make a wish come true. When someone is very sick, people sometimes make a thousand paper cranes to pray for the sick person to get better.

Japanese children also like to play sports—especially baseball.

Besuboru Is "Baseball" in Japanese

The most popular team sport in Japan is baseball, or *besuboru* (bay-soo-boh-roo), which was adopted from the United States in 1873. Baseball is so popular that playing fields must be booked a month or two in advance. People sometimes play as early as six in the morning because that's the only time they can get onto a field!

The Japanese enjoy watching baseball as much as playing it. Each year fifteen million people attend games. There are two major leagues, each with six teams. Outstanding players are heroes in Japan just like in the United States. One baseball hero is Sadaharu Oh, who holds the world record for home runs: 868.

High school baseball is so popular that when the ten-day-long national tournaments are held in spring and summer, practically everyone in the country watches television or listens to the radio to keep up with the game!

Golf is also a popular sport, especially among businessmen. It is very expensive to join a golf club, but companies often pay their managers to entertain business guests by taking them golfing.

45

In recent years skiing has become a popular winter sport. The Winter Olympics were held in Japan in 1972 and will be held there again in 1998. Other popular modern sports are soccer, tennis, volleyball, and ice-skating.

Karate and Judo

Karate and judo are traditional Japanese arts of self-defense that have become popular worldwide. Karate students are trained to concentrate their energy in blows of the hands and feet. Experts can break thick stacks of bricks with one hand. Judo students are taught to turn their opponent's strength back against him or her. Judo is now an Olympic event. Judo and karate train the mind as well as the body.

Kendo, another martial art, is fencing with bamboo swords. It is based on the methods of sword fighting used by the samurai hundreds of years ago. Opponents wear heavy cotton padding and armor so they won't get hurt. Japanese archery, called *kyudo* (kee-yoo-doh), is also popular.

Sumo Wrestling

Sumo wrestling is the oldest sport in Japan. It has been practiced for fifteen hundred years, first at Shinto shrines as part of harvest festivals. It is one of the quickest sports in the world. Two large men weighing hundreds of pounds try to throw each other down or out of a small dirt ring. If any part of the wrestler's body except his feet touches the ground or if he touches the ground outside the ring, he loses. The average match lasts only thirty seconds! Six major tournaments—each with many matches—are held every year before packed audiences.

Before they start, the wrestlers bow to each other, stomp their feet, clap their hands, throw salt into the ring as a symbol

Sumo wrestlers study each other hard before making a move.

of purity, and try to outstare their opponent. Sumo wrestlers train for many years and some become big stars.

Pinballs and Comic Books

Pachinko (pah-cheen-koh) is a pinball game played with small steel balls in a slot machine. The name *pachinko* comes from the sound the balls make when they shoot up into the machine. The purpose is to collect as many balls as possible and turn them in for prizes. More than thirty million Japanese, mostly men, play *pachinko* regularly in thousands of parlors throughout Japan.

Comic books, called *manga* (mahn-gah), are also wildly popular among Japanese of all ages. There are *manga* on every subject: sports, hobbies, history, cooking, and more. It's common to see businessmen, housewives, and young people reading *manga* as they ride the crowded Tokyo subway trains.

A samurai in action. The Japanese people are famous for their woodblock printing, an art form that became popular more than two hundred years ago and is still practiced today. This vivid samurai warrior was cut into a block of wood, painted, and printed about one hundred years ago.

5
THE ARTS

Keeping Ancient
Traditions Alive

In the busy, crowded Japan of today, the Japanese keep their
balance through an emphasis on beauty, simplicity, natural-
ness, and harmony. They practice this attitude in their arts,
crafts, and ancient traditions.

Green Tea and Flowers

The tea ceremony, or *chanoyu* (chah-noh-yoo), is a unique
Japanese art practiced since the fifteenth century. The host pre-
pares and serves green tea and food for guests in a special
small house in a garden. The tearoom is decorated simply with
a single scroll painting or a vase of flowers.

The ceremony, which can last four hours, involves more
than just enjoying a cup of tea. Exact rules must be followed
for everything from the way the tea is stirred to how the cups
are held and turned. The spirit of the tea ceremony is to appreciate the beauty of simplicity and harmony with nature.

Japanese flower arranging, or ikebana (ee-kay-bah-nah), is
another traditional Japanese art. Flowers, leaves, and branches
are arranged in a vase to represent the sky, earth, and people in

harmonious balance. Beautiful flowing lines suggest the season and passage of time. Japanese women study flower arranging along with the tea ceremony and cooking as the three traditional arts wives are expected to know.

Flower arrangements are often displayed in Japanese homes in the special viewing area called the tokonoma. Certain flowers are associated with each holiday. Chrysanthemums are displayed at New Year's, peach blossoms during the Dolls' Festival, and irises on Children's Day.

The tea ceremony, an ancient art that helps people appreciate simplicity and beauty, is held here outdoors.

Haiku and the World's First Novel

The Japanese love of nature is shown in poetry as well as flower arranging. Haiku are very short poems: They have just seventeen syllables arranged in three lines of five, seven, and five syllables each. The season is always named or suggested in haiku. The greatest haiku poet was Bashō, who lived in the seventeenth century.

The world's first major novel was written in Japan in the eleventh century by a lady of the emperor's court named Murasaki Shikibu. *The Tale of Genji* is a fifty-four-volume story of the life of the noblemen and their ladies. Today Japanese literature is known throughout the world for the works of Yasunari Kawabata, who won the Nobel Prize in literature in 1968, and Kenzaburo Oe, who won it in 1994.

Puppets and Masks

Kabuki (kuh-boo-kee), Japan's best-known traditional theater art, has been one of the country's most popular entertainments for three hundred years. The actors wear elaborate costumes and heavy makeup and perform against a backdrop of lavish, colorful scenery. The plays are lively, filled with sword fights, dances, and music. They last about five hours, and people can buy tickets for one or two scenes or for the entire show. Sometimes at the end of the play, the hero stares and crosses his eyes, which is considered a special kind of beauty. Male actors play both male and female roles.

Noh, Japan's oldest theater art, also uses only male actors. The actors wear masks and traditional costumes and move in special, dramatic ways on an almost empty stage. There are five kinds of Noh plays: plays about gods, historical battles, beautiful women, devils, and present-day events. In the days

Kabuki actors on stage in a Tokyo theater. This traditional dramatic art is still very popular in Japan. It is very different from the "natural" kind of acting Westerners are used to.

of the shogun, Noh plays were performed for the wealthy, while Kabuki was for the common people.

Bunraku (boon-rah-koo) is Japanese puppet theater. The puppets are 4 feet (1.22 meters) tall and are operated by three black-robed puppeteers who work on stage. The puppeteers even move the puppets' eyebrows, eyes, and mouths! The story is narrated by one person, who uses different tones of voice for each puppet. The samisen (sah-muh-sehn), a traditional three-stringed instrument, provides music.

A Mix of Music

Besides the samisen, other traditional Japanese instruments are the koto and the *shakuhachi* (shah-koo-hah-chee). The koto is similar to a harp that lies on the floor. It has thirteen strings and is 6 feet (1.82 meters) long. The *shakuhachi* is a bamboo flute that was originally the favorite instrument of wandering Buddhist priests. It has a haunting, beautiful sound. The *shakuhachi*, koto, and samisen are often played together as a trio.

The Japanese also enjoy Japanese popular songs, American popular music, and music from other countries. After work Japanese businessmen often stop by a karaoke (kah-rah-oh-kee) bar. Here they drink, relax, and sing to taped music. No one can get away without a turn at the microphone! Teenagers also like to sing karaoke at parties and youth centers.

Bunraku puppets, gorgeously painted and dressed, and nearly as tall as people, have fascinated Japanese audiences for generations.

Arts, Crafts, and Living Treasures

Woodblock printing is a form of art that became popular in the seventeenth century and that schoolchildren still learn. Woodblock prints are made by carving a picture into a block of wood,

putting paint on the wood, and then pressing the wood onto paper to make a picture. They usually show scenes of nature, daily life, and the theater world. Hokusai was a famous artist who made thirty-six different woodblock prints of Mount Fuji. Many people use woodblock printing to make their own New Year's greeting cards.

Brush painting with black ink on scrolls, painted paper screens, and wood carvings in castles and temples are other examples of Japanese visual arts.

Pottery, textiles, papermaking, and lacquerware are some of Japan's traditional crafts. Lacquering is a method of coating objects with over twenty layers of sap from the Japanese lacquer tree. This gives the objects a glossy, smooth appearance and protects them from moisture. Lacquerware can last for thousands of years. Common lacquerware includes trays, tables, bowls, chopsticks, and tea containers. Even suits of armor have been lacquered! Lacquerware is so closely identified with Japan that the word *japan* itself means "to lacquer."

Artists who become masters at pottery making, metalwork, Kabuki, Noh, and other arts are rewarded by being

Kabuki plays are favorite subjects for works of art. This woodblock print describes a scene from the play Chushingura *in which forty-seven heroes storm a castle.*

55

GARDEN ART

Japan is famous for its gardens. The gardens are small, carefully tended, and designed to be simple but beautiful.

The dry-landscape garden has no plants or trees, just white sand and stones. These gardens were first made by Zen masters, who were also masters of the tea ceremony. The most famous garden of this kind is at Ryoanji, a Zen Temple in Kyoto. It has fifteen stones in a sea of carefully raked white sand.

The hill-style garden contains hills with pine or cherry trees, ponds, and streams. Stepping-stones are placed so the visitor can walk across a stream, and a bridge goes across to an island in a pond. This kind of garden is found near many traditional Japanese temples.

The teahouse garden is a simple garden with stepping-stones leading up to the teahouse. Built with ferns, moss, and evergreen trees and shrubs, the garden is carefully tended to heighten the feeling of peace one gets from the tea ceremony.

Japanese gardens are designed to show nature on a small scale. Another way the Japanese do this is through bonsai, or the art of growing miniature trees. Bonsai trees are created by trimming them closely to shape their growth. Some bonsai trees are only a few inches high and have been handed down within the same family for generations.

named "living national treasures." These master artists receive money from the government so they can teach their arts to others. This way the Japanese traditions continue in each new generation.

Strong and Flexible Like Bamboo

Many of the arts and crafts valued by the Japanese use bamboo. Writing brushes are made of bamboo, as are flower vases, flutes, and fans. The tea ceremony uses bamboo for tea scoops, tea whisks, and water ladles. Bamboo shoots are a common food, and such household items as baskets, placemats, brooms, and chopsticks are made from bamboo. It is said that there are over fourteen hundred uses for bamboo!

One of the many gardens that Japan is famous for. It is easy to see the Japanese love of nature in the simple but beautiful gardens they design.

Bamboo grows wild in Japan. It grows very quickly—as much as 6 feet (1.82 meters) in one week! You can actually watch it grow before your eyes.

Some say bamboo is like the Japanese. It can be bent and stretched into different shapes, but when it is released, it snaps back and continues to grow. When they were exposed to other cultures, the Japanese took the parts they liked and adapted them. And after the destruction in World War II Japan sprang back to become a strong and powerful nation.

Just like the bamboo that they have found so many uses for, the Japanese are flexible and strong, and they continue to grow.

Country Facts

Official Name: Nihon, or Nippon (Japan)

Capital: Tokyo

Location: an island nation off the northeastern coast of Asia, consisting of more than 3,900 islands lying in a chain between the Sea of Japan on the west and the Pacific Ocean on the east. There are four main islands: Hokkaido (hoh-kaid-oh), Honshu (honn-shoo), Shikoku (shih-koh-koo), and Kyushu (kee-oo-shoo). Japan's closest neighbors are Korea and China; both are to the west and separated from Japan by water. The Bonin (boh-nuhn) and the Ryukyu (ree-yoo-kyoo) Islands (Okinawa [oh-kee-nah-wuh] is the largest of the Ryukyus) also belong to Japan.

Area: 145,870 square miles (377,800 square kilometers). *Greatest distances*: east–west, 250 miles (402 kilometers); north–south, 1,865 miles (3,003 kilometers). *Coastline* (the four main islands): 5,857 miles (9,424 kilometers)

Elevation: *Highest:* Mount Fuji, on the island of Honshu, 12,389 feet (3,776 meters) above sea level. *Lowest*: sea level along the coast

Climate: temperate; in the typhoon belt. Summers are warm and humid; winters mild and sunny, except in the north, where they can be very cold with heavy snow.

Population: 125,107,000. *Distribution*: about 77 percent urban, 23 percent rural; nearly all Japanese live on the four largest islands.

Form of Government: Constitutional monarchy; parliamentary democracy headed by prime minister

Important Products: *Natural Resources*: coal, fish, waterpower. *Agriculture*: fruits, rice, tea, vegetables. *Industries*: auto, chemical, electronic, financial, fishing, textile

Basic Unit of Money: yen; l yen = 100 sen

Language: Japanese

Religion: Buddhism; Shinto

Flag: a solid red circle on a white background (called *Hi-no Maru* [hee-noh mah-roo], "Circle of the Sun")

National Anthem: *Kimigayo* ("The Reign of Our Emperor")

Major Holidays: New Year's Day; Coming-of-Age Day, January 15; Commemoration of the Founding of the Nation, February 11; Vernal Equinox Day, March 21; Greenery Day, April 29; Constitution Day, May 3; Children's Day, May 5; Respect-for-the-Aged Day, September 15; Autumnal Equinox Day, September 23; Health-Sports Day, October 10; Culture Day, November 3; Labor-Thanksgiving Day, November 23; Emperor's Birthday, December 23

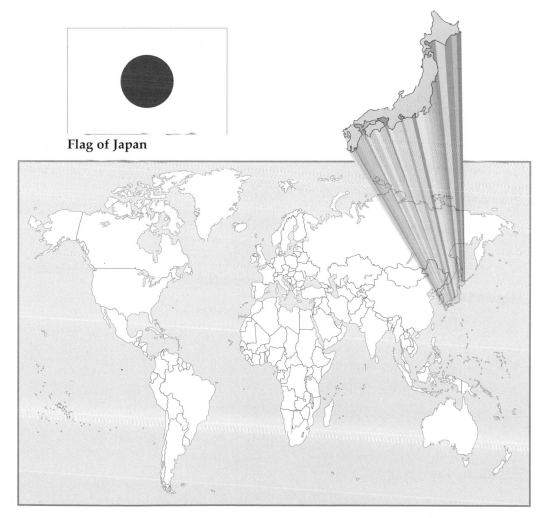

Flag of Japan

Japan in the World

Glossary

Ainu (eye-noo): early settlers of Japan

asa-gohan (ah-sah goh-hahn): breakfast

ban-gohan (bahn goh-hahn): supper

besuboru (bay-soo-boh-roo): baseball

bonsai (bohn-sai): art of growing miniature trees

Bunraku (boon-rah-koo): Japanese puppet theater

calligraphy (kuh-lih-gruh-fee): artistic writing with a brush and ink

chanoyu (chah-noh-yoo): tea ceremony

Diet (dai-eht): Japanese Congress

futon (foo-tahn): cotton mattress

haiku (hai-koo): three-line poem about nature and life

Hina Matsuri (hee-nah mahtsoor-ee): Dolls' Festival celebrated by girls on March 3

hiragana (hihr-ah-gahn-ah): Japanese syllable alphabet

hiru-gohan (hee-roo goh-hahn): lunch

ikebana (ee-kay-bah-nah): art of flower arranging

judo (joo-doh): martial art for self-defense without weapons

Kabuki (kuh-boo-kee): traditional theater form

kanji (kahn-jee): Chinese characters used in written Japanese

karaoke (kah-rah-oh-kee): singing to taped music

karate (kuh-rah-tee): traditional form of unarmed fighting using the hands and feet as weapons

katakana (kah-tah-kah-nah): Japanese syllable alphabet

kendo (kehn-doh): fencing with bamboo swords

kimono (kuh-moh-noh): traditional Japanese robe with wide sleeves

Kodomo-no-hi (koh-doh-moh noh hee): Children's Day festival celebrated on May 5

kotatsu (koh-taht-soo): low table with heater under it

koto (koh-toh): Japanese stringed instrument like a harp

kyudo (kee-yoo-doh): art of Japanese archery

manga (mahn-gah): comic books

martial art (mar-shuhl ahrt): fighting art

meditation (meh-dih-tay-shuhn): focusing one's mind on quiet, peaceful feelings miso (mee-soh): fermented soybean paste

Nihon (nee-hone): name for Japan; also Nippon (neep-ohn); means "land of the rising sun"

Noh (noh): traditional dance-drama

nori (noh-ree): dried seaweed

obi (oh-bee): broad sash worn with kimono

origami (ahr-uh-gah-mee): art of paper folding

O-shogatsu (oh shoh-gaht-soo): New Year's festival

samisen (sah-muh-sehn): musical instrument with three strings, shaped like a banjo

samurai (sah-muh-rai): Japanese warriors

sensei (sehn-say): "master"; Japanese word for teacher

shakuhachi (shah-koo-hah-chee): seven-holed bamboo flute

Shichi-go-san (shee-chee goh sahn): Seven-Five-Three Day; festival celebrated November 15 for children of the ages of three, five, and seven

shogun (shoh-guhn): military ruler of Japan

soba (soh-bah): buckwheat noodle

sumo (soo-moh): traditional Japanese wrestling

surippa (soor-ee-puh): slippers

sushi (soo-shee): vinegared rice topped with raw fish

tatami (tah-tah-mee): straw mat used as floor covering

tempura (tehm-puh-ruh): fish or vegetables fried in batter

tofu (toh-foo): bean curd

tokonoma (toh-kuh-noh-mah): small area in home decorated with scroll painting or vase of flowers

traditional (truh-dish-uhn-uhl): long-established way of doing something

tsunami (tsoo-nah-mee): huge sea waves caused by earthquakes

typhoon (tai-foon): tropical storm

udon (ooh-dahn): noodles made of wheat flour

woodblock printing: pictures made by carving a picture into a block of wood, putting paint on the wood, and then pressing the wood onto paper to make a picture

yukata (yoo-kah-tah): light cotton kimono worn in summer

For Further Reading

Cassedy, Sylvia and Kunihiro Suetake, trans. *Red Dragonfly on My Shoulder.* New York: HarperCollins, 1992.

Cobb, Vicki. *This Place Is Crowded—Japan.* New York: Walker, 1992.

Greene, Carol. *Japan,* Enchantment of the World. Chicago: Children's Press, 1983.

Japan in Your Pocket. 10 volumes. Tokyo: Japan Travel Bureau, 1988.

Japan Today. Tokyo: Japan Graphic, 1992.

Kitamura, Keiji. *Origami Animals.* Tokyo: Graph-sha Ltd., 1994.

Martin, Rafe. *Ghostly Tales of Japan* (audiocassette). Cambridge, Massachusetts: Yellow Dog Press, 1989.

Martin, Rafe. *Mysterious Tales of Japan.* New York: G. P. Putnam's Sons, Spring 1996.

Montroll, John. *Easy Origami.* New York: Dover, 1992.

Pitts, Forrest Ralph. *Japan.* Grand Rapids, Michigan: Gateway Press, 1988.

Shelley, Rex. *Japan,* Cultures of the World. New York: Marshall Cavendish, 1994.

Uchida, Yoshiko. *The Magic Listening Cap: More Folk Tales from Japan.* Berkeley: Creative Arts Book Company, 1987.

Yagawa, Sumiko. *The Crane Wife.* New York: William Morrow, 1981.

Zurlo, Tony. *Japan: Superpower of the Pacific.* New York: Dillon Press, 1991.

Index

About the Author

Irene Flum Galvin has been fascinated by Japan ever since she fell in love with haiku at the age of ten. Her favorite haiku poet is Bashō, who wrote:

An old silent pond,
into the pond a frog jumps,
splash! silence again.

To prepare to write this book, the author took a class in Japanese, listened to Japanese *shakuhachi* music, and ate many lunches at a Japanese restaurant, where she tried out her new language skills on unsuspecting waiters and waitresses.

Irene Flum Galvin's books for young readers include *Chile: Land of Poets and Patriots* and *The Rubber Band Boy.* She also writes magazine articles and novels. She speaks Spanish and French and has a master's degree from Harvard University. Ms. Galvin is the president of the Communications Connection, a writing and editorial services company in Rochester, New York, where she lives with her husband, Tom, and two children.